Oh no,
POEMS!!!

NOTHING BEATS
A PIZZA

Written and illustrated
by Loris Lesynski

Wait a minute.
WAIT A MINUTE.
Maybe something GOOD
is in it!

annick press
toronto • vancouver • new york

For my sister Lena

©2001 Loris Lesynski (text and art)
Third printing, August 2006

Annick Press Ltd.

We acknowledge the support of the Canada Council for the Arts, the Ontario Arts Council, and the Government of Canada through the Book Publishing Industry Development Program (BPIDP) for our publishing activities.

Cataloging in Publication Data

Lesynski, Loris
   Nothing beats a pizza

Poems.
ISBN 1-55037-701-9 (bound)
ISBN 1-55037-700-0 (pbk.)

I. Title.

PS8573.E79N67 2001   jC811'.54   C2001-930080-8
PZ7.L47No 2001

Distributed in Canada by:
Firefly Books Ltd.
66 Leek Crescent
Richmond Hill, ON
L4B 1H1

Published in the U.S.A. by:
Annick Press (U.S.) Ltd.

Distributed in the U.S.A. by:
Firefly Books (U.S.) Inc.
P.O. Box 1338
Ellicott Station
Buffalo, NY 14205

Printed and bound in Canada by Friesens, Altona, Manitoba.

The art in this book was rendered in colored pencil, watercolor, house paint, tomato sauce, eyeshadow, rubber stamp-pad ink, and ordinary pencil.

The text was typeset in Utopia and Syntax with some other fonts doing guest appearances. The ones that look like handwriting are called Lemonade and Zemke Hand. The title on the cover is in Klunder.

Check out Loris' website at www.lorislesynski.com for tons of ideas, poems, news, etc.

Visit us at:
www.annickpress.com

reading without pizzazz

reading out loud with pizzazz

INGREDIENTS

INTRO

A *picture* of a sandwich
    isn't really like a sandwich
        and you wouldn't feel too full
            when you were done.

A ball, if you just hold it,
    never threw it,
    never rolled it,
isn't really like a ball
that's any fun.

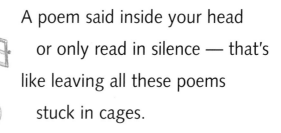

A poem said inside your head
    or only read in silence — that's
like leaving all these poems
    stuck in cages.

But **read aloud**, with noises,
    made by you, the girls and boyses —
then you'll hear them leap right off
    the pages.

Nothing Beat-beat-beats A Pizza

Nothing beats a pizza
when you're in a pizza mood
because a pizza isn't anything
like any other food

other food is neat and tidy
pizza's slippy pizza's slidey

*(makes me full and satisfied-y
nicest slices now inside me)*

Make a pizza
bake a pizza
take a pizza home
eat a pizza in a group or
on your own.

When we want to eat a pizza
then it's better having two
'cuz just one pizza's not enough
for me and you
and you
and you
and you and you and YOU.

Pizza's cheesy pizza's chewy
pizza's gooey pizza's good
(really slow beat)

Pizza'scheesypizza'schewypizza'sgooeypizza'sgood
(really fast beat)

Nothing Beats a Poem

Nothing beats a poem
when you're in a
poem mood because
you never know
exactly what a poem
might include.
It offers laughs
and often thoughts
and pictures in your head,
and sometimes says,
"Let's look at things this
other way instead."

Make a poem bake a poem
take a poem home
write a pizza poem
in a group or on your own.

5

Bizzy Boys

Busy boys are bumping thumping
  clumping down the halls.
Busy boys are stamping stomping
  tromping up the walls.
Yelling boys are making noises—
  don't get in the way!
And what are they so busy at?
  They're going out to play.

"Hey!" cried the buffalo.
  "What's that noise?
I think I heard
  a herd of boys!"

A Guy's Gotta Move

A guy's gotta move
  like he knows where to go
a guy's gotta move
with an ebb and a flow
a guy's gotta know
  when to stand
  when to glide
a guy's gotta know
  inside

Backwards Max

Backwards Max comes down the hall
 as fast and straight
 as a bowling ball
 but in *reverse*
and he stays upright!
 Did Max rehearse at home last night?
 We have to laugh,
 though the teacher glares.
 What's going to happen —
 what's going to happen —
 what's going to happen
 when he hits the stairs?

Backwards Me, Backwards You

I write my name down backwards.
 Who would that person be?
Some other someone
 as totally different from me as
 you ever did see.

Write your own name backwards.
 Who would *that* person be?

loves writing
likes kids
afraid of
mean dogs
laughs a lot
not very tidy
loves music

Loris Lesynski

wears icky colors
snarls a lot
extremely neat
likes turnip
sings on key
goes skydiving

Sirol Iksnysel

7

Too Many Amandas

On the very first day of school they came
>*ta da*
>>*ta da.*

Twenty-one girls with the very same name
>*ta da*
>>*ta da.*

They came in pairs up the halls and stairs,
they filled up most of the classroom chairs,
all of them saying the name was theirs,
>>*ta da   ta da*
>>>*ta da   ta da   ta da.*

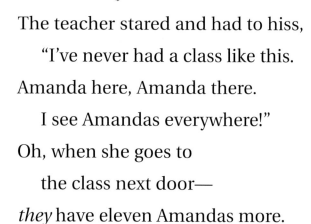

The teacher stared and had to hiss,
>"I've never had a class like this.

Amanda here, Amanda there.
>I see Amandas everywhere!"

Oh, when she goes to
>the class next door—

they have eleven Amandas more.

One Amanda

One Amanda,
   two Amanda,
     three Amanda, four.
Five Amandas come a-marching
 through the classroom door.
Six Amanda, seven Amanda,
   eight and nine and ten.
How will the rest of us *ever* remember
   which is which of them?
Tall Amanda,
   Math Amanda,
Amanda who lost her boot.
   Amanda with freckles, Amanda B.,
Amanda who plays the flute.
   Amanda who has a basset hound,
Amanda allergic to peas.
   Two Amandas who make us laugh,
and seven Amanda G's.

I Look in the Mirror

I look in the mirror
   and what do I see?
Someone that everyone else
   calls me.
This is my hair. This is my nose.
   These are my shoulders,
   and these are my clothes.
They see me, they know me,
   they call out my name.
They seem to believe that
   I'm always the same.
But none of my dreams or
   my thoughts can be seen.
You can see what I look like
   but not what I mean.
Look at me closely with
   all of your eyes —
   all you will see is
   my perfect disguise.

Pizza Theme & Variations

To fry up a frightful witches' pizza,
choose between spiders and bugs.
Melt eye of newt and
tongue of toad,
and sprinkle it with slugs.

A dragon can toss a pizza high
in the air with a flip of his tail,
cook it fast with a blast of flame,
and eat it with ginger ale.

You're fired!

Jack was a pizza delivery boy
till the day of the Giant's call.
Jack couldn't balance the "party size"
on a beanstalk quite so tall.

Porridge too hot?

Porridge too cold?

The story of Goldilocks *could*

be told

with pizza.

"Papa Bear's pizza?

Not enough cheese.

Mama's has too many

anchovies.

But Baby Bear's pizza?

The best in the wood!"

Said Goldie, "It's almost

un*bear*ably good

pizza."

Princesses' pizzas in days of old were royal circles of scarlet and gold.

Forsooth! My pizza doth be cold!

11

Pizza with
1 topping · 2 toppings · 3 toppings
or
EVERYTHING

"Everything"

A pizza with "everything on it"?
I want it I want it I want it!
But I wonder . . . does "everything"
mean the same thing
to everyone else as me?

Choices

"Everything"?
Moon pizza sprinkled
with golden stars
and swirls of tomato-clouds
straight from Mars.

"Everything"?
May I suggest
mice
on every slice?

The candy-lover's
pizza wish?
Jelly beans,
chocolate,
and licorice.
"Everything"
is not complete
(sugar, more sugar!)
unless it's
sweet.

Oh, children......

Mock Pizza

Imitation mozzarella
    powdered pepperoni
the crust is just like cardboard so
    you know the dough is phony

fake salami
    oily sauce
        onions dehydrated
old tomatoes
    bacon bits
        cheese-like substance grated

        deep-dish pizza?
        cheap pizza
        cheddar pizza?
        cheater pizza

pizza-maker, what's the deal?
pizza-faker, make it real
        odd pizza?
        fraud pizza!
not-inside-MY-body pizza!

Bet it's not
fantastic pizza.
Bet it's
tastes-like-plastic pizza.

INSTANT
PIZZA!
Artificial
Ingredients

Mud pies, bro?

Mud pizzas,
to go!

13

Old, Cold Pizza

Old, cold pizza.

   Having breakfast all alone.

Everybody's gone to work.

   There's only me at home.

Wish that someone else was here.

   Pizza, could you say:

"Morning, kid — I hope you have

   a really awesome day."

Once Upon a Time-ee-o

Once upon a time-ee-o
  (begins this little rhyme-ee-o),
a mommio and daddio
  were all alone
  and sad-ee-o,
and so they thought
that maybe-o
  they'd have a little baby-o.

The baby-o was you-ee-o,
  their little honeydew-ee-o,
once so sweet and small-ee-o,
  but now so big and tall-ee-o.

And like the other kiddee-os,
  you're into sports and videos
and like to bike and race-ee-o
  and go from place to place-ee-o,
talk-talk-talk on the phone-ee-o
then read and be alone-ee-o
or hang out with the guys-ee-o.

Kitchy coo!

But in your parents' eyes-ee-o
you're still their little bunny-ee-o,
  so even though it's funny-o,
just *let* them reminisce*-ee-o.
  (And every once in a while-ee-o,
  although it's juvenile-ee-o,
  but just to make them smile-ee-o,
  let 'em *hug and kiss-ee-o*.)

*REMINISCE (rem-i-**niss**) means when people go on and on about the past and how wonderful it was and how cute you were as a baby.

15

What I'd Like to Know

Do teachers ever giggle?

Do teachers ever drool?

Do teachers ever wish
they didn't have to
go to school?

Do teachers ever end up spending
recess all alone?

Do teachers ever miss me when
I'm sick and
staying home?

When teachers get together with
their friends at half past three,
do teachers have as good a time
as all my friends and me?

No Smirchling Allowed

A brand new teacher came today
   from one of the other schools.
"Be serious," she ordered us,
   "and listen to my rules.

"There won't be any splurching,
   and you're not allowed to flitz.
Anybody caught klumpeting
   will put me in a snitz.

"No floozering at recess.
   Grufflinking's not permitted.
And anyone who splubs outside
   will *not* be readmitted.

"When you put your hand up,
   I don't want to hear a bloud.

And let's be clear that while
   I'm here, no sneeping is allowed."

I was truly baffled, but I didn't
   want to show it.
What if I was flitchering and
   didn't even know it?

We sat as still as statues.
   None of us made a peep.
All of us were terrified
   we'd accidentally sneep.

We didn't have a *clue* about
   the rules that she was using.
How can anyone be good
   when being good is so confusing?

THE CLEAN DOG
Boogie

"Too messy!" said our mother
   when we asked her for a pet.
But then we saw a sign for one
   we knew she'd let us get:
"Guaranteed — the cleanest dog
   the world has ever known."
Just the pet we wanted!
   We had to take him home.

It started in the car: he tried to lick
   the windshield clean.
"What a helpful puppy," said our
   mother, "what a dream."
In the house, he polished all
   the doorknobs with his tongue,
then used his snout to vacuum, getting
   every single crumb.
He licked the dusty lampshades. He slurped the dirty walls.
   He chased the dusty bunnies up and down the dusty halls.
His ears were perfect dishrags, his tail a built-in broom.
   He soaked himself in soapsuds and he rolled around the room.

18

But then — he *ate* the lampshades,
  licked the photo albums blank.
Found the dish detergent,
  every drop of which he drank.
He swallowed up a scatter rug
  while lapping at the edge.
Books and houseplants toppled as
  he swept the window ledge.

"Take him out!" our mother said.
  We didn't question why.
He slobbered on the seesaw.
  He sucked the sandbox dry.
Then he licked the baby's head
  and made her even balder.
Where's the pet shop owner's card?
  Right away I called her.

Dog-lips cleaned the phone as I
  described the situation.
"Sort of an… experiment,"
  she said in explanation.
"But check his head: the seventh
  brownish freckle near the top—
that's the switch." I found it.
  Instantly, he stopped.

Once he was a cleaning machine,
  now he's a regular mutt.
We're delighted to have him the way
  he is, a conventional canine,
  BUT…
when my room gets dusty,
as it does every now and then,
  I'd almost like to find that switch
    and turn him on again.

Ruby

Ruby wakes up full of pounce
    and instantly begins to bounce:
playing catching growling chasing
    darting jumping running racing,
skittering up and down the halls,
    chewing shoes and bones and balls,
pretending a hat is an enemy rat,
    shaking it, making it ragged and flat.
    Then suddenly — down on the floor she'll plop,
no pause at all between GO and STOP,
    and right in the middle of a *yap-yap-yap*
she's sound asleep in an instant nap:
    that's what puppies do.

Sigh...lence

The foss...

　　foss...

　　　faucet's

　　　　dripping...

　　　　　*plink...plink...plink*ing in the sink...

and the kitchen clock is ticking ... it's so quiet, who can think?

**I can only do my homework
when there's music noise and sound,
when there's barking boiling talking,
when the house is really rocking, for
my brain is trained to do its best
with racket all around!**

So now...

　　how can...

　　　I concentrate...

on spelling or subtracting?

　　This silent...

　　　peaceful...

　　　　atmosphere...

　　　　　is *totally* distracting.

21

The Bad Mood Blues

You *wake* up in the morning and
you *know* it's there

BAD M O O O D

BAD M O O O D

From underneath the covers
you can feel it in the air

BAD M O O O D

BAD M O O O D

22

Everything goes wrong the day
you wake up in the dumps
you know your socks have vanished
and your hair has gone in clumps
      your milk is spilling everywhere
      your brother has to *poke* you
      and everybody's bugging you
      and says it's just a *joke,* you
        know it isn't fair and know
        you're totally upset
        and the *day* hasn't even
          the *day* hasn't even
          the *day* hasn't even

S T A R T E D   Y E T

so whatcha gonna do
when you wake up feeling blue
gotta figure out a way to
get a rhythm to the day

and B E A T B E A T B E A T

B E A T B E A T B E A T

B E A T B E A T B E A T the

BAD MOOD away.

Buster's Scat Singing

When you've got the mulligrubs
when you're feeling low
When you're just a sourpuss and
no one wants to know you
you gotta have a place inside
that's always good to go to
somewhere down inside you where
you're happy smart and wise, and
there's dancing in the street, and
there's music in the skies
then instead of feeling draggy
feeling crabby, feeling glum,
you can rise above the grumbles
and have some fun.

Taste Buds

"WHAT'S IN YOUR MOUTH?" asks the substitute teacher.
Everyone's staring at Bonzo McFee.

Taste buds for sour
taste buds for sweet
taste buds for bitter things awful to eat
taste buds for salty
like popcorn and chips
waste buds when Brussels sprouts
cross your lips

He stops in the middle of chewing and answers
(ever so sweetly), "Well now, let me see:

there are glands for saliva,

there's all of my teeth,

molars, incisors,

with gums underneath.

One epiglottis,

one palate,

one tongue.

At the back of my throat there's

a uvula hung.

Over ten thousand taste buds

and millions of cells.

Is that what you wanted to know,

Mrs. Wells?"

The regular teacher

    knows Bonzo loves gum.

And also smart answers.

    And playing dumb.

He wouldn't question. *He* wouldn't shout.

    He'd say very simply, "Spit *all* of it out."

We 🖤 Sour!

Mike likes pickles
more than pie.
So do I. So do I.
Keeps sour candies
in good supply.
So do I. So do I.
Maybe our tongues
are missing some
of the taste buds meant
for candy and gum?
Lemons and onions
and relish and pickles,
green apples and
mustard —
yum!

Where
does all the air
inside the bubbles of my
P O P
wallow when I swallow
and the fizzing has to
stop?

Lately I've Been Late

Lately I've been
  late a lot.
    Is this some *disease*
      I've got?
        I've become so
          very
           slow
             just can't get myself
             to go
             want to wait
              and want to stall
             lots to look at
              watch it all
           clocks are ticking
             everywhere
          don't much notice
            don't much care
         sometimes time
           is slow and sweet
        I've got a case
          of summer feet.

Cloud Pizza

Look, the clouds
are arranged today,
it seems to me,
in a pizza-shaped way,
but take a bite and
you'd have to say,
*"Sky pizza, air pizza,
tastes like nothing-there
pizza."*

Play Ball!

High ball, low ball, fast ball, slow ball, curve ball, swerve ball, straight ball, great ball!

Morning O'Clock

Summertime means
I don't have to know
how many minutes
still to go.
It's morning o'clock
when the sun comes by
and we run together across the sky,
sail over meadows, leap over lakes,
swing rock to rock for
as long as it takes.
It's evening o'clock
when we sleep, and then
it's morning o'clock again.

Leaves

Leaves were here

they left their prints

in greenish grayish brownish tints

like rubber stamps along the road

an autumn message left in code

Pizzas were here.
They left their
crumbs...

28

No Two Snowflakes

No two snowflakes
are the same.
That's what gives them
all that fame.
But what about potatoes?
What about peas?
What about you's
and what about me's?
They're not identical.
They're not so similar.
Snowflakes aren't really more
incredible than these.

No two pizzas
are the same...

Snowman Pizza

Snowman pizza must have just
   a plain and simple ice cream crust
with snowflake sauce in an icy glop
   and grated icicle bits on top.
But this is one pizza you'd never bake.
   Imagine the size of the puddle you'd make!

29

How Sam Eats

Sam eats his sandwiches
all round the edges,
biting the sides away fast.
He says that the centers
are best in his
sandwiches.
That's why
he saves them
for last.

"It's not scientific.
It's all the same sandwich.
The middle is just like
the rest" —
that's what we all said
before we gave
sandwiches
Sam's Sandwich Center
Taste Test.

The pointy part of pizza
is the bit
that tastes the best.
I'll nibble
at the little tips
and you can eat
the rest.

You're driving me crazy!!!

Good Advice

Never **ever** sit beside
   a picky pizza eater.
They're always so suspicious, what
   they'll like and what they won't.
Finicky, they pull off bits
   not sure to be delicious.
And do they mind the choosing?
   No, they don't.

Never **ever** sit beside
   a picky poem writer.
They're always fussing with the words
   to make a poem brighter.
Adding here, erasing there, to get
   it right. They really care.
And will they ever bother less?
   They won't.

You're driving me crazy!!!

Dear Reader

If *Nothing Beats A Pizza*
makes you hungry for your own,
   if you want to write a story,
     if you want to write a poem,
       then play with words and say with words
       what's shaking in your mind.
   Imagination makes the writing really fun to find.
       Any idea begins it. Any idea can cook.
         Now *go*, dear adorable reader —
        you've come to the end of this book.

FOOTNOTES

Answers to the Most Frequently Asked Questions:

- Why "pizza"? The author admits that *she's*
  in love with *zzzz*-zy sounds like these.
  Enjoy these poems, but be on guard:
  your lips may fall off if you read them too hard.

- No, a poem does not *have to* rhyme to be a poem.

- Yes, there are more books like this in the works.

THE END

Name	Amount	Weight g	Energy calories	Protein g	Carb. g	Fiber g	Total fat g	Sat. fat g	Chol. mg	Sod. mg	Vit. A RE	Vit. C mg	Calc. mg	Iron mg
Fruit cocktail, light syrup	½ cup	121	69	0.5	18.1	1.2	0.1	0	0	7	12	2.3	7	0.4
Fruit cocktail, juice	½ cup	119	55	0.5	14.1	1.2	0	0	0	5	18	3.2	9	0.3
Grapefruit	½ medium	128	41	0.8	10.3	1.4	0.1	0	0	0	59	44.0	15	0.1
Grapefruit juice	¾ cup	185	70	1.0	16.6	0.2	0.2	0	0	2	2	54.1	13	0.4
Grapes	12 grapes	60	41	0.4	10.9	0.6	0.1	0	0	1	2	6.5	6	0.2
Guava	1 fruit	90	46	0.7	10.7	4.9	0.5	0.2	0	3	28	165.2	18	0.3
Honeydew	⅛ melon, 5¼" dia.	125	44	0.6	11.5	1.0	0.1	0	0	13	5	22.5	8	0.2
Kiwifruit	1 large	91	56	0.9	13.5	3.1	0.4	0	0	5	8	68.3	24	0.4
Kumquats	5 fruits	95	67	1.8	15.1	6.2	0.8	0.1	0	10	14	41.7	59	0.8
Lemon, with peel	1 fruit	108	22	1.3	11.6	5.1	0.3	0	0	3	3	83.2	66	0.8
Lemon juice	2 tablespoons	31	8	0.1	2.6	0.1	0	0	0	6	0	14.0	2	0
Mango	½ medium	103	65	0.5	17.0	1.8	0.3	0.1	0	2	39	28.7	10	0.1
Nectarine	1 fruit	136	60	1.4	14.4	2.3	0.4	0	0	0	23	7.3	8	0.4
Olives, ripe	10 large	44	51	0.3	2.8	1.4	4.7	0.6	0	383	9	0.4	39	1.5
Orange	1 medium	131	62	1.2	15.4	3.1	0.2	0	0	0	14	69.7	52	0.1
Orange juice	¾ cup	186	84	1.3	19.3	0.4	0.4	0	0	2	19	93	20	0.4
Papaya	½ medium	152	59	0.9	14.9	2.7	0.2	0.1	0	5	84	93.9	36	0.2
Passion fruit	½ cup	118	114	2.6	27.6	12.3	0.8	0.1	0	33	76	35.4	14	1.9
Peach, raw	1 medium	98	38	0.9	9.3	1.5	0.2	0	0	0	16	6.5	6	0.2
Peach, canned in juice	½ cup	124	55	0.8	14.3	1.6	0	0	0	5	24	4.4	7	0.3
Pear, raw	1 medium	166	98	0.6	25.1	4.0	0.7	0	0	0	3	6.6	18	0.4
Pear, canned	½ cup	124	62	0.4	16.0	2.0	0.1	0	0	5	0	2.0	11	0.4
Persimmon, raw	1 fruit	25	32	0.2	8.4	0	0.1	0	0	0	0	16.2	7	0.6
Pineapple, canned in juice	½ cup	125	75	0.5	19.5	1.0	0.1	0	0	1	2	11.8	17	0.3
Pineapple, raw	1 slice, 3½" x 3¼"	84	40	0.5	10.6	1.2	0.1	0	0	1	3	30.4	11	0.2
Plantain, raw	1 medium	179	218	2.3	57.1	4.1	0.6	0.3	0	7	100	32.9	5	1.1
Plums	1½ medium	99	46	0.7	11.3	1.4	0.3	0	0	0	17	9.4	6	0.2
Prune juice	¾ cup	192	136	1.2	33.5	1.9	0.1	0	0	8	0	7.9	23	2.3
Prunes (dried plums)	5 prunes	42	101	0.9	26.8	3.0	1.2	0	0	1	16	0.3	18	0.4
Raisins	¼ cup	41	123	1.3	32.7	1.5	1.2	0	0	5	0	0.9	21	0.8
Raspberries	½ cup	62	32	0.7	7.3	4.0	0.4	0	0	1	1	16.1	15	0.4
Rhubarb, raw	1 stalk	51	11	0.5	2.3	0.9	0.1	0	0	2	3	4.1	44	0.1
Strawberries	5 large	90	27	0.6	6.3	2.1	0.3	0	0	1	1	51.0	13	0.3
Tangerine	1 medium	84	37	0.5	9.4	1.9	0.2	0	0	1	29	25.9	12	0.1
Watermelon	1/16 melon	286	86	1.7	21.6	1.1	0.4	0	0	3	80	23.2	20	0.7

MILK, YOGURT, AND CHEESE

The Food Guide Pyramid recommends 2–3 servings per day. One serving is equivalent to 1 cup milk or yogurt, 1½ ounces of natural cheese, or 2 ounces of processed cheese.

Name	Amount	Weight g	Energy calories	Protein g	Carb. g	Fiber g	Total fat g	Sat. fat g	Chol. mg	Sod. mg	Vit. A RE	Vit. C mg	Calc. mg	Iron mg
Buttermilk, lowfat	1 cup	245	98	8.1	11.7	0	2.2	1.3	10	257	17	2.5	284	0.1
Cheese, American	2 oz.	57	188	11.1	4.7	0	13.9	8.8	36	548	90	0	282	0.5
Cheese, blue	1½ oz.	43	150	9.1	1.0	0	12.2	7.9	32	593	84	0	225	0.1
Cheese, cheddar	1½ oz.	43	171	10.6	0.5	0	14.1	9.0	45	264	113	0	307	0.3
Cheese, cottage, creamed	1 cup	210	216	26.2	5.6	0	9.5	6.0	32	850	92	0	126	0.3
Cheese, cottage, lowfat (1%)	1 cup	226	163	28.0	6.1	0	2.3	1.5	9	918	25	0	138	0.3
Cheese, cottage, non-fat	1 cup	145	123	25.0	2.7	0	0.6	0.4	10	19	13	0	46	0.3
Cheese, cream	2 oz.	57	198	4.3	1.5	0	19.8	12.5	62	168	208	0	45	0.7
Cheese, cream, fat free	2 oz.	57	55	8.2	3.3	0	0.8	0.5	5	311	159	0	105	0.1
Cheese, feta	1½ oz.	43	112	6.0	1.7	0	9.0	6.4	38	475	54	0	210	0.3
Cheese, Mexican	1½ oz.	43	151	9.6	1.2	0	12.0	7.6	45	279	23	0	281	0.2
Cheese, Monterey	1½ oz.	43	159	10.4	0.3	0	12.9	8.1	38	228	84	0	317	0.3
Cheese, mozzarella (part skim)	1½ oz.	43	108	10.3	1.2	0	6.8	4.3	27	263	54	0	333	0.1
Cheese, Parmesan, grated	2 tablespoons	10	43	3.9	0.4	0	2.9	1.7	9	153	12	0	111	0.1
Cheese, process spread	2 oz.	56	170	9.1	5.5	0	12.3	8.1	45	839	100	0.1	261	0.1
Cheese, provolone	1½ oz.	43	149	10.9	0.9	0	11.3	7.3	29	373	100	0	321	0.2
Cheese, ricotta, part skim	½ cup	124	171	14.1	6.4	0	9.8	6.1	38	155	133	0	337	0.5
Cheese, Swiss	1½ oz.	43	160	12.1	1.4	0	11.7	7.6	39	111	94	0	409	0.1
Ice cream, chocolate	1 cup	132	285	5.0	37.2	1.6	14.2	9.0	45	100	157	0.9	144	1.2
Ice cream, vanilla, rich	1 cup	214	533	7.5	47.7	0	34.7	22.1	197	131	389	0	250	0.7

Name	Amount	Weight g	Energy calories	Protein g	Carb. g	Fiber g	Total fat g	Sat. fat g	Chol. mg	Sod. mg	Vit. A RE	Vit. C mg	Calc. mg	Iron mg
Ice cream, vanilla, light	1 cup	146	241	7.8	39.0	0.4	5.8	3.8	36	108	201	0.3	169	0.1
Ice cream, vanilla, soft-serve	1 cup	172	382	7.0	1.2	1.2	22.4	12.9	157	105	279	1.4	225	0.4
Milk, chocolate	1 cup	250	208	7.9	25.9	2.0	8.5	5.3	30	150	65	2.3	280	0.6
Milk, fat free (nonfat)	1 cup	245	86	8.4	11.9	0	0.4	0.3	5	127	149	2.5	301	0.1
Milk, lowfat (1%)	1 cup	244	102	8.0	12.1	0	2.4	1.6	12	107	144	2.4	290	0.1
Milk, reduced fat (2%)	1 cup	244	122	8.1	11.7	0	4.7	2.9	20	122	139	2.4	298	0.1
Milk, whole	1 cup	244	146	7.9	11.0	0	7.9	4.6	24	98	68	0	276	0.1
Pudding, chocolate	½ cup	147	163	4.6	27.6	1.5	4.6	2.7	16	417	38	1.3	150	0.4
Yogurt, frozen, vanilla	1 cup	144	235	5.8	34.9	0	8.1	4.9	3	125	85	1.2	206	0.4
Yogurt, lowfat, plain	8 oz. container	227	143	11.9	16.0	0	3.5	2.3	14	159	32	1.8	415	0.2
Yogurt, lowfat, with fruit	8 oz. container	227	238	11.0	42.2	0	3.2	2.1	14	148	36	1.6	384	0.2
Yogurt, nonfat, plain	8 oz. container	227	127	13.0	17.4	0	0.4	0.3	5	175	5	2.0	452	0.2

MEAT, POULTRY, FISH, DRY BEANS, EGGS, AND NUTS

The Food Guide Pyramid recommends 2–3 servings per day for a total of 5–7 ounces. One serving is equivalent to 2–3 ounces of cooked lean meat, poultry, or fish. The following count as equivalents of 1 ounce of meat: ½ cup of cooked dry beans or tofu, 2½ ounces of soyburger, 1 egg, 2 tablespoons of peanut butter, ⅓ cup of nuts, or ¼ cup of seeds.

Name	Amount	Weight g	Energy calories	Protein g	Carb. g	Fiber g	Total fat g	Sat. fat g	Chol. mg	Sod. mg	Vit. A RE	Vit. C mg	Calc. mg	Iron mg
Bacon, Canadian	2 slices	47	86	11.3	0.6	0	3.9	1.3	27	727	0	0	5	0.4
Beef, ½" fat	3 oz.	85	344	19.9	0	0	28.7	11.9	78	48	0	0	9	2.1
Beef, lean, fat trimmed	3 oz.	85	179	25.4	0	0	7.9	3.0	73	56	0	0	7	2.5
Beef, corned	3 oz.	85	213	23.0	0	0	12.7	5.3	73	856	0	0	10	1.8
Beef, ground, extra lean, broiled	3 oz.	85	218	21.6	0	0	13.9	5.5	71	60	0	0	6	2.0
Beef, ground, lean, broiled	3 oz.	85	231	21.0	0	0	15.7	6.2	74	65	0	0	9	1.8
Beef, ground, regular, broiled	3 oz.	85	246	20.5	0	0	17.6	6.9	77	71	0	0	9	2.1
Beef liver, braised	3 oz.	85	137	20.7	2.9	0	4.2	1.6	331	60	9011	19.6	6	5.8
Beef ribs, broiled	3 oz.	85	306	18.7	0	0	25.1	10.2	70	53	0	0	10	1.8
Chicken breast, w/skin, rst	½ breast	98	193	29.2	0	0	7.6	2.1	82	70	26	0	14	1.0
Chicken, dk mt, w/skin, rst	3 oz.	85	215	22.1	0	0	13.4	3.7	77	74	49	0	13	1.2
Chicken, dk mt, w/o skin, rst	3 oz.	85	168	22.2	0	0	7.9	2.2	76	76	18	0	12	1.1
Chicken, dk mt, w/skin, fried	3 oz.	85	253	18.6	8.0	0	15.8	4.2	76	251	26	0	18	1.2
Chicken, drumstick, w/skin, rst	1 drumstick	52	112	14.1	0	0	5.8	1.6	47	47	16	0	6	0.7
Chicken, lt mt, w/skin, rst	3 oz.	85	189	24.7	0	0	9.2	2.6	71	64	27	0	13	1.0
Chicken, lt mt, w/o skin, rst	3 oz.	85	147	26.3	0	0	3.8	1.1	72	65	8	0	13	0.9
Chicken, lt mt, w/skin, fried	3 oz.	85	235	20.0	8.1	0	13.1	3.5	71	243	20	0	17	1.1
Chicken, thigh, w/skin, rst	1 thigh	62	153	15.5	0	0	9.6	2.7	58	52	30	0	7	0.8
Chicken, wing, w/skin, rst	1 wing	34	99	9.1	0	0	6.6	1.9	29	28	16	0	5	0.4
Chicken liver, chopped	½ cup	70	110	17.1	0.8	0	3.8	1.3	442	36	3439	11.1	10	5.9
Egg white, large	1 egg white	33	17	3.5	0.3	0	0	0	0	55	0	0	2	0
Egg, whole, large	1 egg	50	75	6.2	0.6	0	5.1	1.6	213	63	97	0	25	0.7
Egg yolk, large	1 yolk	17	55	2.8	0.3	0	5.1	1.6	213	7	97	0	23	0.6
Fish, catfish, baked/broiled	3 oz.	85	129	15.9	0	0	6.8	1.5	54	68	13	0.7	8	0.7
Fish, cod, baked/broiled	3 oz.	85	89	19.5	0	0	0.7	0.1	47	66	9	2.6	7	0.3
Fish, halibut, baked/broiled	3 oz.	85	119	22.7	0	0	2.5	0.4	35	59	46	0	51	0.9
Fish, salmon, baked/broiled	3 oz.	85	175	18.8	0	0	10.5	2.1	54	52	13	3.1	13	0.3
Fish, salmon, canned	3 oz.	85	130	17.4	0	0	6.2	1.4	37	457	45	0	203	0.9
Fish, salmon, smoked	3 oz.	85	99	15.5	0	0	3.7	0.8	20	666	22	0	9	0.7
Fish, sardine, canned in oil	1 can (3.75 oz.)	92	191	22.7	0	0	10.5	1.4	131	465	62	0	351	2.7
Fish, snapper, baked/broiled	3 oz.	85	109	22.3	0	0	1.5	0.3	40	48	30	1.4	34	0.2
Fish sticks	3 sticks	84	228	13.1	19.9	0	10.3	2.6	94	489	26	0	17	0.6
Fish, swordfish, baked/broiled	3 oz.	85	132	21.6	0	0	4.4	1.2	43	98	35	0.9	5	0.9
Fish, trout, baked/broiled	3 oz.	85	162	22.6	0	0	7.2	1.3	63	57	16	0.4	47	1.6
Fish, tuna, canned in oil	3 oz.	85	158	22.6	0	0	6.9	1.4	26	337	4	0	3	0.6
Fish, tuna, canned in water	3 oz.	85	109	20.1	0	0	2.5	0.7	36	320	5	0	12	0.8
Ham, extra lean	3 oz.	85	116	18.0	0.4	0	4.1	1.4	26	965	0	0	5	0.8
Ham, regular	3 oz.	85	192	17.5	0.4	0	12.9	4.3	53	800	0	11.9	7	1.2
Lamb, trimmed	3 oz.	85	218	20.8	0	0	14.3	6.7	74	65	0	0	14	1.6
Lunch meat, beef pastrami	3 oz.	85	297	14.7	2.6	0	24.8	8.9	79	1043	0	0	8	1.6

Name	Amount	Weight g	Energy calories	Protein g	Carb. g	Fiber g	Total fat g	Sat. fat g	Chol. mg	Sod. mg	Vit. A RE	Vit. C mg	Calc. mg	Iron mg
Lunch meat, beef, sliced	3 oz.	85	151	23.9	4.9	0	3.3	1.4	35	1224	0	0	9	2.3
Lunch meat, bologna (beef)	3 slices	85	265	10.4	0.7	0	24.2	10.3	49	834	0	0	10	1.4
Lunch meat, bologna (turkey)	3 slices	85	169	11.7	0.8	0	12.9	4.3	84	747	0	0	71	1.3
Lunch meat, chicken breast	3 oz.	85	108	14.3	1.9	0	4.7	1.2	50	1005	0	0	14	1.3
Lunch meat, franks (beef)	1 frank	57	180	6.8	1.0	0	16.2	6.9	35	585	0	0	11	0.8
Lunch meat, franks (chicken)	1 frank	45	116	5.8	3.1	0	8.8	2.5	45	617	17	0	43	0.9
Lunch meat, ham, lean, sliced	3 slices	85	111	16.5	0.8	0	4.2	1.4	40	1215	0	0	6	0.6
Lunch meat, liverwurst	3 oz.	85	277	12.0	1.9	0	24.2	9.0	134	731	7066	0	22	5.4
Lunch meat, salami, dry	8 slices	80	326	18.3	1.3	0	27.5	9.8	63	1808	0	0	10	1.2
Lunch meat, turkey, smoked	3 oz.	85	85	15.0	2.0	0	2.0	0.5	36	781	0	0	8	0.6
Meatloaf (80% lean meat)	3 oz.	85	216	21.5	0	0	13.7	5.2	76	57	0	0	20	2.2
Nuts, almonds	⅓ cup	47	274	10.1	9.3	5.6	24.0	1.8	0	0	0	0	117	2.0
Nuts, cashews, dry roasted	⅓ cup	46	262	7.0	14.9	1.4	21.2	4.2	0	7	0	0	21	2.7
Nuts, chestnuts, roasted	⅓ cup	48	117	1.5	25.2	2.4	1.0	0.2	0	1	1	12.4	14	0.4
Nuts, macadamia, dry roasted	⅓ cup	45	321	3.5	6.0	3.6	34.0	5.3	0	2	0	0.3	31	0.3
Nuts, pecans	⅓ cup	36	249	3.3	5.0	3.5	25.9	2.2	0	0	2	0.4	25	0.9
Nuts, pine	⅓ cup	45	300	6.1	5.8	1.6	30.5	2.2	0	1	0	0.4	7	2.5
Nuts, pistachios, dry roasted	⅓ cup	43	244	9.1	11.8	4.4	19.6	2.4	0	4	23	1.0	47	1.8
Nuts, walnuts	⅓ cup	41	255	9.9	4.1	2.8	24.3	1.4	0	1	1	0.7	25	1.3
Peanut butter, chunky	2 tablespoons	32	190	8.3	5.7	1.8	16.5	3.2	0	117	375	0	17	5.6
Peanut butter, smooth	2 tablespoons	32	190	8.1	6.2	1.9	16.3	3.3	0	149	0	0	12	0.6
Peanuts, dry roasted	⅓ cup	45	269	7.8	11.5	4.1	23.3	3.1	0	5	0	0.2	32	1.7
Pork chop, pan fried	3 oz.	85	190	23.5	0	0	10.0	3.7	60	44	2	0.3	4	0.7
Pork ribs, braised	3 oz.	85	252	20.3	0	0	18.3	6.8	74	50	2	0.6	25	1.0
Pork roast	3 oz.	85	214	22.9	0	0	12.9	4.5	69	41	3	0	5	0.8
Pumpkin seeds, roasted	¼ cup	57	296	18.7	7.6	2.2	23.9	4.5	0	10	22	1.0	24	8.5
Sausage, beef	1 sausage	43	134	6.1	1.0	0	11.6	4.9	29	486	0	0	3	0.8
Sausage, pork	1 link	68	265	15.1	1.4	0	21.6	7.7	46	1020	0	1.4	20	0.8
Sausage, smoked links	3 2" links	48	161	6.4	0.7	0	14.6	5.1	34	454	0	0	5	0.7
Shellfish, clams, canned	3 oz.	85	126	21.7	4.4	0	1.7	0.2	57	95	154	18.8	78	23.8
Shellfish, clams, steamed	10 clams	95	140	24.3	4.9	0	1.9	0.2	64	106	162	21.0	87	26.6
Shellfish, crab, steamed	3 oz.	85	82	16.4	0	0	1.3	0.1	45	911	8	6.5	50	0.6
Shellfish, oysters, fried	6 medium	88	173	7.7	10.2	0	11.1	2.8	71	367	79	3.3	55	6.1
Shellfish, shrimp, canned	3 oz.	85	102	19.6	0.9	0	1.7	0.3	147	144	15	2.0	50	2.3
Shellfish, shrimp, fried	4 large	30	73	6.4	3.4	0.1	3.7	0.6	53	103	17	0.5	20	0.4
Sunflower seeds, dry roasted	¼ cup	32	186	6.2	7.7	3.6	15.9	1.7	0	1	0	0.4	22	1.2
Tempeh	½ cup	83	160	15.4	7.8	0	9.0	1.8	0	7	0	0	92	2.2
Tofu, firm	½ cup	126	183	19.9	5.4	2.9	11.0	1.6	0	18	10	0.3	861	13.2
Turkey, dk mt, w/o skin, rst	3 oz.	85	138	24.5	0	0	3.7	1.2	95	67	0	0	22	2.0
Turkey, dk mt, w/skin, rst	3 oz.	85	155	23.5	0	0	6.0	1.8	99	65	0	0	23	2.0
Turkey, lt mt, w/o skin, rst	3 oz.	85	119	25.7	0	0	1.0	0.3	73	48	0	0	13	1.3
Turkey, lt mt, w/skin, rst	3 oz.	85	139	24.5	0	0	3.9	1.1	81	48	0	0	15	1.4
Veal, sirloin, roasted	3 oz.	85	172	21.4	0	0	8.9	3.8	87	71	0	0	11	0.8
Vegetarian bacon, cooked	1 oz.	16	50	1.7	1.0	0.4	4.7	0.7	0	234	1	0	4	0.4
Vegetarian franks	1 frank	51	118	12.1	1.5	1.5	7.1	0.8	0	224	0	0	10	1.0
Vegetarian patties	1 patty	67	119	11.2	10.2	4.0	3.8	0.5	0	382	76	0	48	1.2
Vegetarian sausage	1 patty	38	97	7.0	3.7	1.1	6.9	1.1	0	337	24	0	24	1.4

FATS, OILS, SWEETS, AND ALCOHOLIC BEVERAGES

The total amount of fats, oils, and sweets you consume should be determined by your overall energy needs. Foods from this group should not replace foods from the other groups because they tend to provide calories but few nutrients.

Name	Amount	Weight g	Energy calories	Protein g	Carb. g	Fiber g	Total fat g	Sat. fat g	Chol. mg	Sod. mg	Vit. A RE	Vit. C mg	Calc. mg	Iron mg
Alcoholic beverage, beer	1 can or bottle	356	146	1.1	13.2	0.7	0	0	0	14	0	0	18	0.1
Alcoholic beverage, liquor	1.5 oz.	42	97	0	0	0	0	0	0	0	0	0	0	0
Alcoholic beverage, wine	5 oz.	148	106	0.3	2.5	0	0	0	0	7	0	0	12	0.6
Bacon	3 slices	24	126	9.1	0.4	0	9.6	3.2	27	575	3	0	3	0.3
Beverage, fruit punch	1 cup	247	114	0	28.9	0.2	0	0	0	10	2	108.4	10	0.2

Name	Amount	Weight g	Energy calories	Protein g	Carb. g	Fiber g	Total fat g	Sat. fat g	Chol. mg	Sod. mg	Vit. A RE	Vit. C mg	Calc. mg	Iron mg
Beverage, cola	1 can	370	155	0	39.7	0	0	0	0	15	0	0	11	0.1
Beverage, lemon-lime soda	1 can	368	147	0	38.3	0	0	0	0	40	0	0	7	0.3
Beverage, tea, bottled, sweetened	1 bottle	480	178	0	40.8	0	0	0	0	0	0	0	0	0
Butter	1 tablespoon	14	102	0.1	0	0	11.5	7.1	31	82	97	0	3	0
Candy, caramels	1 piece	10	39	0.5	7.8	0.1	0.8	0.7	1	25	1	0.1	14	0
Candy, fudge	1 piece	17	70	0.4	13	0.3	1.8	1.0	2	8	7	0	8	0.3
Candy, jelly beans	10 large	28	104	0	26.4	0	0.1	0	0	7	0	0	1	0.3
Candy, milk chocolate	1 bar	44	235	3.4	26.1	1.5	13.1	6.3	10	35	22	0	83	1.0
Chocolate syrup	2 tablespoons	39	109	0.8	25.4	1.0	0.4	0.2	0	28	0	0.1	5	0.8
Cream, half and half	2 tablespoons	30	39	0.9	1.3	0	3.5	2.2	11	12	29	0.3	32	0
Cream, heavy, whipped	½ cup	60	206	1.2	1.7	0	22.1	13.8	82	23	247	0.4	39	0
Cream, sour	1 tablespoon	12	26	0.4	0.5	0	2.5	1.6	5	6	21	0.1	14	0
Frosting, chocolate	2 tablespoons	41	163	0.5	25.9	0.4	7.2	2.3	0	75	0	0	3	0.6
Honey	1 tablespoon	21	64	0.1	17.3	0	0	0	0	1	0	0.1	1	0.1
Jam/preserves	1 tablespoon	20	56	0.1	13.8	0.2	0	0	0	6	0	1.8	4	0.1
Lard	1 tablespoon	13	115	0	0	0	12.8	5.0	12	0	0	0	0	0
Marmalade, orange	1 tablespoon	20	49	0.1	13.3	0	0	0	0	11	1	1.0	8	0
Margarine, regular stick	1 tablespoon	14	99	0	0.3	0	11.0	2.1	0	92	115	0	0	0
Margarine, liquid	1 tablespoon	14	102	0.3	0	0	11.4	1.9	0	111	113	0	9	0
Margarine, soft	1 tablespoon	14	101	0.1	0	0	11.3	2.0	0	152	113	0	4	0
Margarine-like spread	1 tablespoon	14	50	0.1	0.1	0	5.6	1.1	0	138	118	0	3	0
Mayonnaise, regular	1 tablespoon	15	57	0.1	3.5	0	4.9	0.7	4	105	12	0	2	0
Mayonnaise, fat free	1 tablespoon	16	11	0	2.0	0.3	0.4	6.1	2	120	1	0	1	0
Oil, canola	1 tablespoon	14	124	0	0	0	14.0	1.0	0	0	0	0	0	0
Oil, corn	1 tablespoon	14	120	0	0	0	13.6	1.7	0	0	0	0	0	0
Oil, olive	1 tablespoon	14	119	0	0	0	13.5	1.8	0	0	0	0	0	0.1
Popsicle	1 single stick	88	63	0	16.6	0	0	0	0	11	0	9.4	0	0
Salad dressing, blue cheese	2 tablespoons	31	154	1.5	2.3	0	16.0	3.0	5	335	20	0.6	25	0.1
Salad dressing, French	2 tablespoons	32	146	0.3	5.0	0	14.3	1.8	0	268	7	0	8	0.3
Salad dressing, Italian	2 tablespoons	29	86	0.1	3.1	0	8.3	1.3	0	486	1	0	2	0.2
Salad dressing, Italian, light	2 tablespoons	30	32	0	1.5	0	2.9	0.4	2	236	0	0	1	0.1
Sherbet	½ cup	74	107	0.8	22.5	0	1.5	0.9	0	34	7	2.3	40	0.1
Shortening, vegetable	1 tablespoon	13	115	0	0	0	12.8	5.2	0	0	0	0	0	0
Sugar, brown	1 tablespoon	14	52	0	13.4	0	0	0	0	5	0	0	12	0.3
Sugar, white	1 tablespoon	13	49	0	12.6	0	0	0	0	0	0	0	0	0
Syrup, corn	1 tablespoon	20	56	0	15.3	0	0	0	0	24	0	0	1	0
Syrup, maple	¼ cup	79	206	0	52.9	0	0.2	0	0	7	0	0	53	0.9

DATA SOURCE: U.S. Department of Agriculture, Agricultural Research Service. 2004. *USDA Nutrient Database for Standard Reference, Release 16.1* (http://www.nal.usda.gov/fnic/foodcomp).

Arby's

	Serving size	Calories	Protein	Total fat	Saturated fat	Total carbohydrate	Sugars	Fiber	Cholesterol	Sodium	Vitamin A	Vitamin C	Calcium	Iron	% calories from fat
	g		g	g	g	g	g	g	mg	mg		% RDI			
Regular roast beef	157	350	21	16	6	34	N/A	2	85	950	N/A	0	6	20	41
Super roast beef	245	470	22	23	7	47	N/A	3	85	1130	N/A	2	8	20	44
French dip	285	440	28	18	8	42	N/A	2	100	1680	N/A	2	8	25	37
Junior roast beef	129	310	16	13	4.5	34	N/A	2	70	740	N/A	0	6	15	38
Roast chicken Caesar sandwich	363	820	43	38	9	75	N/A	5	140	2160	N/A	15	35	25	42
Roast turkey & Swiss	360	760	43	33	6	75	N/A	5	130	1920	N/A	4	35	25	39
Chicken breast fillet	208	540	24	30	5	47	N/A	2	90	1160	N/A	6	8	10	50
Hot ham 'n Swiss sandwich	170	340	23	13	4.5	35	N/A	1	90	1450	N/A	2	15	15	34
Jalapeño bites™	111	330	7	21	9	30	N/A	2	40	670	N/A	2	4	4	57
Cheddar curly fries	170	460	6	24	6	54	N/A	4	5	1290	N/A	25	6	10	47
Potato cakes (2)	100	250	2	16	4	26	N/A	3	0	490	N/A	10	0	4	58
Grilled chicken Caesar salad	338	230	33	8	3.5	8	N/A	3	80	920	N/A	70	20	10	31
Thousand Island dressing	57	290	1	28	4.5	9	N/A	0	35	480	N/A	0	0	0	87
French-toastix	124	370	7	17	4	48	N/A	4	0	440	N/A	0	7	10	41

N/A: not available.

SOURCE: Arby's © 2004, Arby's, Inc. (http://www.arbysrestaurant.com). Used with permission of Arby's, Inc. Nutritional information contained in this Arby's, Inc. brochure was obtained from independent lab analysis, Genesis Nutrition and Diet Software, supplier information, and the USDA Handbook #8. Information on Arby's products contained herein is based on laboratory and calculated analysis of Arby's ingredients as of April 2004. Actual nutritional information may differ based on regional variability in product availability and in individual unit compliance with Arby's Standard Operating Procedures. Information is not to be used by individuals with special dietary needs in lieu of professional medical advice.

Burger King

	Serving size	Calories	Protein	Total fat	Saturated fat	Trans fat	Total carbohydrate	Sugars	Fiber	Cholesterol	Sodium	Vitamin A	Vitamin C	Calcium	Iron	% calories from fat
	g		g	g	g	g	g	g	g	mg	mg		% Daily Value			
Original WHOPPER®	291	700	31	42	13	1	52	8	4	85	1020	20	15	10	30	54
Original WHOPPER® w/o mayo	270	540	30	24	10	1	52	8	4	75	900	10	15	10	30	40
Original DOUBLE WHOPPER® w/cheese	399	1060	56	69	27	3	53	9	4	185	1540	25	15	30	45	59
Original WHOPPER JR.®	158	390	17	22	7	0.5	31	5	2	45	550	10	6	8	15	51
BK VEGGIE® Burger*	186	380	14	16	2.5	0	46	6	4	5	930	15	6	8	35	38
Chicken WHOPPER®	272	570	38	25	4.5	0	48	5	4	75	1410	15	10	6	40	39
CHICKEN TENDERS® (8 pieces)	123	340	22	19	5	3.5	20	0	<1	50	840	2	0	2	4	50
French fries (medium, salted)	117	360	4	18	5	4.5	46	1	4	0	640	0	15	2	4	45
Onion rings (medium)	91	320	4	16	4	3.5	40	5	3	0	460	0	0	10	0	45
Chili (w/o cheese or crackers)	217	190	13	8	3	0	17	5	5	25	1040	25	60	8	8	38
Fire-grilled chicken caesar salad (w/o dressing or toast)	286	190	25	7	3	0	9	1	1	50	900	80	40	15	8	33
CROISSAN'WICH® w/bacon, egg, and cheese	119	360	15	22	8	2	25	4	<1	195	950	8	0	30	20	55
HERSHEY®'S sundae pie	79	300	3	18	10	1.5	31	23	1	10	190	2	0	4	6	54
Chocolate Shake (medium)	397	600	10	18	11	0	97	94	2	70	470	15	6	45	8	27

* Burger King Corporation makes no claim that the BK VEGGIE® Burger or any of its products meets the requirements of a vegan or vegetarian diet.

SOURCE: BURGER KING® nutritional information used with permission from Burger King Brands, Inc.

Domino's Pizza

(1 serving = 2 of 8 slices or ¼ of 14-inch pizza; 2 of 8 slices or ¼ of 12-inch pizza; 1 6-inch pizza)

	Serving size g	Calories	Protein g	Total fat g	Saturated fat g	Total carbohydrate g	Sugars g	Fiber g	Cholesterol mg	Sodium mg	Vitamin A	Vitamin C	Calcium	Iron	% calories from fat
											% Daily Value				
14-inch lg. hand-tossed cheese	219	516	21	15	7	75	6	4	32	1080	18	0	26	23	26
14-inch lg. thin crust cheese	148	382	17	17	7	43	6	2	32	1172	18	0	32	8	40
14-inch lg. deep dish cheese	256	677	26	30	11	80	9	5	41	1575	21	<1	33	31	40
12-inch med. hand-tossed cheese	159	375	15	11	5	55	5	3	23	776	13	0	19	17	26
12-inch med. thin crust cheese	106	273	12	12	5	31	4	2	23	835	13	0	23	5	40
12-inch med. deep dish cheese	181	482	19	22	8	56	6	3	30	1123	15	<1	24	22	41
Toppings: pepperoni	*	98	5	9	3	<1	<1	<1	20	364	<1	<1	<1	2	83
ham	*	31	5	2	<1	<1	<1	<1	12	292	<1	<1	<1	1	58
Italian sausage	*	110	5	9	3	3	<1	<1	22	342	<1	<1	2	3	74
bacon	*	153	8	13	4	<1	<1	<1	22	424	0	15	<1	2	77
beef	*	111	6	10	4	<1	<1	<1	21	309	<1	0	<1	3	81
anchovies	*	45	9	2	<1	<1	<1	<1	18	791	<1	0	5	6	40
extra cheese	*	68	6	6	3	<1	<1	<1	15	228	6	0	12	<1	79
cheddar cheese	*	71	5	6	3	<1	<1	<1	18	110	4	0	13	<1	76
Barbeque buffalo wings (1 piece)	25	50	6	2	<1	2	1	<1	26	175	<1	<1	<1	2	36
Buffalo chicken kickers™ (1 piece)	24	47	4	2	<1	3	<1	<1	9	163	0	0	<1	0	38
Blue cheese sauce	42	223	1	23	4	2	2	<1	20	417	1	0	2	<1	93
Breadsticks (1 stick)	37	116	3	4	<1	18	1	1	0	152	<1	<1	<1	5	31
Double cheesy bread	43	142	4	6	2	18	<1	1	6	183	2	<1	5	5	38

* Topping information is based on minimal portioning requirements for one serving of a 14-inch large pizza; add the values for toppings to the values for a cheese pizza. The following toppings supply fewer than 15 calories per serving: green and yellow peppers, onion, olives, mushrooms, pineapple.

SOURCE: Domino's Pizza, 2004 (http://www.dominos.com). Reproduced with permission from Domino's Pizza LLC.

Jack in the Box

	Serving size g	Calories	Protein g	Total fat g	Saturated fat g	Total carbohydrate g	Sugars g	Fiber g	Cholesterol mg	Sodium mg	Vitamin A	Vitamin C	Calcium	Iron	% calories from fat
											% Daily Value				
Breakfast Jack®	129	310	13	14	5	33	4	1	205	720	N/A	N/A	N/A	N/A	42
Supreme croissant	171	570	19	37	9	41	5	1	240	1040	N/A	N/A	N/A	N/A	58
Hamburger	119	310	17	14	6	30	6	1	45	600	N/A	N/A	N/A	N/A	42
Jumbo Jack® w/cheese	314	690	27	38	16	61	13	3	70	1360	N/A	N/A	N/A	N/A	49
Sourdough Jack®	244	700	30	49	16	36	7	3	80	1220	N/A	N/A	N/A	N/A	63
Chicken fajita pita	230	330	24	11	4.5	35	4	3	55	910	N/A	N/A	N/A	N/A	30
Sourdough grilled chicken club	249	520	33	28	6	33	5	3	85	1330	N/A	N/A	N/A	N/A	48
Ultimate club	316	640	37	30	9	51	7	3	105	2000	N/A	N/A	N/A	N/A	42
Jack's Spicy Chicken®	308	730	30	37	10	69	9	4	70	1480	N/A	N/A	N/A	N/A	45
Monster taco	119	260	9	15	5	21	4	3	30	340	N/A	N/A	N/A	N/A	50
Egg rolls (3)	170	400	14	19	6	44	4	6	15	920	N/A	N/A	N/A	N/A	43
Chicken breast pieces (5)	150	360	27	17	3	24	0	1	80	970	N/A	N/A	N/A	N/A	43
Stuffed jalapeños (7)	168	530	15	30	13	51	5	4	45	1600	N/A	N/A	N/A	N/A	51
Barbeque dipping sauce	28	45	0	0	0	11	4	0	0	330	N/A	N/A	N/A	N/A	0
Seasoned curly fries	125	400	6	23	5	45	1	5	0	890	N/A	N/A	N/A	N/A	52
Onion rings	119	500	6	30	5	51	3	3	0	420	N/A	N/A	N/A	N/A	54
Side salad	137	50	3	3	1.5	4	2	2	10	65	N/A	N/A	N/A	N/A	54
Thousand Island dressing	57	160	0	12	2	12	10	0	15	490	N/A	N/A	N/A	N/A	68
Oreo® cookie ice-cream shake (16 oz)	301	670	11	33	19	81	62	1	110	350	N/A	N/A	N/A	N/A	45

N/A: not available.

SOURCE: Jack in the Box, Inc. 2003 (http://www.jackinthebox.com). The following trademarks are owned by Jack in the Box, Inc.: Breakfast Jack,® Jumbo Jack,® Sourdough Jack,® Jack in the Box.® Reproduced with permission from Jack in the Box, Inc.

KFC

	Serving size g	Calories	Protein g	Total fat g	Saturated fat g	Total carbohydrate g	Sugars g	Fiber g	Cholesterol mg	Sodium mg	Vitamin A	Vitamin C	Calcium	Iron	% calories from fat
											% Daily Value				
Original Recipe® breast	161	380	40	19	6	11	0	0	145	1145	0	0	0	6	45
Original Recipe® thigh	126	360	22	25	7	12	0	0	165	1060	0	0	0	6	63
Extra Crispy™ breast	162	460	34	28	8	19	0	0	135	1230	0	0	0	8	55
Extra Crispy™ thigh	114	370	21	26	7	12	0	0	120	710	0	0	0	6	63
Hot & Spicy breast	179	460	33	27	8	20	0	0	130	1450	0	0	0	6	53
Hot & Spicy thigh	128	400	22	28	8	14	0	0	125	1240	0	0	0	8	63
Tender Roast® sandwich w/sauce	196	390	31	19	4	24	0	1	70	810	0	0	4	10	44
Tender Roast® sandwich w/o sauce	177	260	31	5	1.5	23	0	1	65	690	0	0	4	10	17
Hot Wings™ pieces (6)	134	450	24	29	6	23	1	1	145	1120	6	6	8	10	58
Colonel's Crispy Strips® (3)	151	400	29	24	5	17	0	0	75	1250	0	6	0	10	54
Popcorn chicken (large)	170	660	29	44	10	37	0	0	75	1530	0	4	4	35	60
Chicken pot pie	423	770	33	40	15	70	2	5	115	1680	200	0	0	20	47
Corn on the cob (5.5")	162	150	5	3	1	26	10	7	0	10	0	10	6	6	18
Mashed potatoes w/gravy	136	120	2	4.5	1	18	<1	1	0	380	2	4	0	2	34
BBQ baked beans	136	230	8	1	1	46	22	7	0	720	8	6	15	30	4
Cole slaw	130	190	1	11	2	22	13	3	5	300	25	40	4	0	52
Biscuit (1)	57	190	2	10	2	23	1	0	1.5	580	0	0	0	4	47
Potato salad	128	190	2	11	2	22	5	1	5	470	0	10	0	2	52

SOURCE: KFC Corporation, 2004 (http://www.kfc.com). Reproduced with permission from Kentucky Fried Chicken Corporation.

Subway
Based on standard formulas with
6-inch subs on Italian or wheat bread

	Serving size g	Calories	Protein g	Total fat g	Saturated fat g	Total carbohydrate g	Sugars g	Fiber g	Cholesterol mg	Sodium mg	Vitamin A	Vitamin C	Calcium	Iron	% calories from fat
											% Daily Value				
Italian BMT®	248	450	23	21	8	47	8	4	55	1790	10	35	15	20	42
Meatball Marinara	287	500	23	22	11	52	9	5	45	1180	10	40	15	35	40
Subway® Seafood Sensation	255	380	16	13	4.5	52	8	5	25	1170	10	35	15	20	31
Cheese steak	256	360	24	10	4.5	47	9	5	35	1090	10	35	15	40	25
Turkey breast, ham & bacon melt	260	380	25	12	5	47	8	4	45	1610	10	35	15	20	28
Classic tuna	255	430	20	19	5	46	7	5	45	1070	10	35	15	20	40
Sweet onion chicken teriyaki	266	370	26	5	1.5	58	18	4	50	1100	8	45	8	20	12
Honey mustard ham	243	310	19	5	1.5	54	14	5	25	1410	8	35	6	20	15
Roast beef	222	290	19	5	2	45	8	4	20	910	8	35	6	30	16
Turkey breast, ham & roast beef	255	320	24	6	2	47	8	4	35	1300	8	35	6	30	17
Savory turkey breast	222	280	18	4.5	1.5	46	7	4	20	1010	8	35	6	20	14
Veggie Delite®	166	230	9	3	1	44	7	4	0	510	8	35	6	20	12
Savory turkey breast deli	151	210	13	3.5	1.5	36	4	3	15	730	6	20	6	20	15
Chicken Bacon Ranch Wrap	215	480	40	27	9	19	3	11	95	1340	6	15	40	10	51
Bacon and egg breakfast sandwich	123	320	15	15	4.5	34	3	3	185	520	6	6	8	20	42
Garden fresh salad w/ Seafood Sensation (w/o dressing or toppings)	380	210	10	11	3.5	20	7	5	25	740	160	80	20	10	47
Garden fresh salad	300	60	3	1	0	11	5	5	0	80	160	80	8	10	15
New England clam chowder	240	110	5	3.5	0.5	16	1	1	10	990	2	0	10	0	29
Chili con carne	240	240	15	10	5	23	14	8	15	860	15	0	6	6	38
Sunrise refresher (small)	341	120	1	0	0	29	28	1	0	20	4	210	2	0	0
Choclate chip cookie	45	210	2	10	4	30	18	1	15	160	4	0	0	6	43

SOURCE: Subway U.S. Nutrition Info as found on http://www.subway.com, 4/23/2004. Reprented by permission of Subway.

Taco Bell

	Serving size (g)	Calories	Protein (g)	Total fat (g)	Saturated fat (g)	Total carbohydrate (g)	Sugars (g)	Fiber (g)	Cholesterol (mg)	Sodium (mg)	Vitamin A	Vitamin C	Calcium	Iron	% calories from fat
											% Daily Value				
Taco	78	170	8	10	4	13	1	3	25	350	6	4	6	6	53
Taco Supreme®	113	220	9	14	7	14	.2	3	40	360	10	8	8	8	57
Soft taco, beef	99	210	10	10	4.5	21	2	2	25	620	6	4	10	10	43
Soft Taco Supreme,® chicken	134	230	15	10	5	21	3	1	45	570	8	8	15	6	39
Gordita Supreme,® steak	153	290	16	13	6	28	7	2	35	520	6	6	10	15	37
Gordita Baja,® chicken	153	320	17	15	3.5	29	7	2	40	690	6	6	10	10	42
Chalupa Supreme, beef	153	390	14	24	10	31	5	3	40	600	10	8	15	10	55
Chalupa Supreme, chicken	153	370	17	20	8	30	4	1	45	530	6	8	10	6	49
Bean burrito	198	370	14	10	3.5	55	4	8	10	1200	10	8	20	15	24
Burrito Supreme,® chicken	248	410	21	14	6	50	5	5	45	1270	15	15	20	15	31
Grilled stuffed burrito, beef	325	730	28	33	11	79	7	10	55	2080	20	10	35	25	41
Tostada	170	250	11	10	4	29	2	7	15	710	10	8	15	8	36
Zesty Chicken Border Bowl™ w/dressing	417	730	23	42	9	65	5	12	45	1640	20	15	15	20	52
Taco salad with salsa	533	790	31	42	15	73	10	13	65	1670	30	35	40	35	48
Steak quesadilla	184	540	26	31	14	40	4	3	70	1370	15	0	50	15	52
Nachos Supreme	195	450	13	26	9	42	4	7	35	800	8	10	10	10	58
Nachos BellGrande®	308	780	20	43	13	80	6	12	35	1300	10	10	20	15	50
Pintos 'n cheese	128	180	10	7	3.5	20	1	6	15	700	10	6	15	6	35
Mexican rice	131	210	6	10	4	23	<1	3	15	740	20	8	10	10	43

SOURCE: Taco Bell Corporation, 2003 (http://www.tacobell.com). Reproduced courtesy of Taco Bell Corporation.

Wendy's

	Serving size (g)	Calories	Protein (g)	Total fat (g)	Saturated fat (g)	Trans fat (g)	Total carbohydrate (g)	Sugars (g)	Fiber (g)	Cholesterol (mg)	Sodium (mg)	Vitamin A	Vitamin C	Calcium	Iron	% calories from fat
												% Daily Value				
Classic Single® w/everything	218	410	25	19	7	1	37	8	2	70	910	N/A	N/A	N/A	N/A	42
Big Bacon Classic®	282	580	33	29	12	1.5	45	11	3	95	1430	N/A	N/A	N/A	N/A	45
Jr. hamburger	117	270	15	9	3.5	0.5	34	7	2	30	610	N/A	N/A	N/A	N/A	30
Jr. bacon cheeseburger	165	380	20	19	7	1	34	6	2	55	830	N/A	N/A	N/A	N/A	45
Ultimate Chicken Grill Sandwich	225	360	31	7	1.5	0	44	11	2	75	1100	N/A	N/A	N/A	N/A	18
Spicy Chicken Fillet Sandwich	225	510	29	19	3.5	1.5	57	8	2	55	1480	N/A	N/A	N/A	N/A	34
Homestyle Chicken Fillet Sandwich	230	540	29	22	4	1.5	57	2	2	55	1320	N/A	N/A	N/A	N/A	37
Caesar side salad (no toppings or dressing)	99	70	6	4.5	2	0	2	1	1	10	190	N/A	N/A	N/A	N/A	58
Chicken BLT salad (no toppings or dressing)	376	360	34	19	9	0.5	10	4	4	95	1140	N/A	N/A	N/A	N/A	48
Taco Supremo salad (no toppings or dressing)	495	360	27	16	8	1	29	8	8	65	1090	N/A	N/A	N/A	N/A	40
Creamy ranch dressing	64	230	1	23	4	0.5	5	3	0	15	580	N/A	N/A	N/A	N/A	90
Reduced fat creamy ranch dressing	64	100	1	8	1.5	0	6	3	1	15	550	N/A	N/A	N/A	N/A	72
Biggie® fries	159	440	5	19	3.5	5	63	0	7	0	380	N/A	N/A	N/A	N/A	39
Baked potato w/broccoli & cheese	411	440	10	15	3	0	70	6	9	10	540	N/A	N/A	N/A	N/A	31
Baked potato w/bacon & cheese	380	560	16	25	7	0	67	6	7	35	910	N/A	N/A	N/A	N/A	40
Chili, small, plain	227	200	17	5	2	0	21	5	5	35	870	N/A	N/A	N/A	N/A	23
Chili, large w/cheese	357	370	29	13	6.5	0	32	7	7	65	1420	N/A	N/A	N/A	N/A	32
Crispy Chicken Nuggets™ (5)	75	220	10	14	3	1.5	13	0	0	35	490	N/A	N/A	N/A	N/A	57
Barbecue sauce (1 packet)	28	40	1	0	0	0	10	5	0	0	160	N/A	N/A	N/A	N/A	0
Frosty,™ medium	298	430	10	11	7	0	74	55	0	45	200	N/A	N/A	N/A	N/A	23

SOURCE: Wendy's International, Inc., 2004 (http://www.wendys.com). Reproduced with permission from Wendy's International, Inc.

Information on additional foods and restaurants is available online; see the Web sites listed with the tables in this appendix and the following additional sites:
Hardees: http://www.hardees.com   **McDonald's:** http://www.mcdonalds.com   **White Castle:** http://www.whitecastle.com

Monitoring Your Progress

NAME _____ SECTION _____ DATE _____

As you completed the 13 labs listed below, you entered the results in the Preprogram Assessment column of this lab. Now that you have been involved in a fitness and wellness program for some time, do the labs again and enter your new results in the Postprogram Assessment column. You will probably notice improvement in several areas. Congratulations! If you are not satisfied with your progress thus far, refer to the tips for successful behavior change in Chapter 1 and throughout this book. Remember—fitness and wellness are forever. The time you invest now in developing a comprehensive, individualized program will pay off in a richer, more vital life in the years to come.

	Preprogram Assessment	Postprogram Assessment
LAB 2.2 Activity Profile	Sleep: _____ hours Light activity: _____ hours Moderate activity: _____ hours Vigorous activity: _____ hours Stairs climbed: _____ flights	Sleep: _____ hours Light activity: _____ hours Moderate activity: _____ hours Vigorous activity: _____ hours Stairs climbed: _____ flights
LAB 3.1 Cardiorespiratory Endurance 1-mile walk test 3-minute step test 1.5-mile run-walk test	$\dot{V}O_{2max}$: _____ Rating: _____ $\dot{V}O_{2max}$: _____ Rating: _____ $\dot{V}O_{2max}$: _____ Rating: _____	$\dot{V}O_{2max}$: _____ Rating: _____ $\dot{V}O_{2max}$: _____ Rating: _____ $\dot{V}O_{2max}$: _____ Rating: _____
LAB 4.1 Muscular Strength Maximum bench press test Maximum leg press test Hand grip strength test	Weight: _____ lb Rating: _____ Weight: _____ lb Rating: _____ Weight: _____ kg Rating: _____	Weight: _____ lb Rating: _____ Weight: _____ lb Rating: _____ Weight: _____ kg Rating: _____
LAB 4.2 Muscular Endurance Curl-up test Push-up test	Number: _____ Rating: _____ Number: _____ Rating: _____	Number: _____ Rating: _____ Number: _____ Rating: _____
LAB 5.1 Flexibility Sit-and-reach test	Score: _____ cm Rating: _____	Score: _____ cm Rating: _____

	Preprogram Assessment	Postprogram Assessment
LAB 5.3 Low-Back Muscular Endurance Side bridge endurance test Trunk flexors endurance test Back extensors endurance test	Right: _____ sec Rating: _____ Left: _____ sec Rating: _____ Trunk flexors: _____ sec Rating: _____ Back extensors: _____ sec Rating: _____	Right: _____ sec Rating: _____ Left: _____ sec Rating: _____ Trunk flexors: _____ sec Rating: _____ Back extensors: _____ sec Rating: _____
LAB 6.1 Body Composition Body mass index Skinfold measurements (or other method for determining percent body fat) Waist circumference Waist-to-hip-circumference ratio	BMI: _____ kg/m^2 Rating: _____ Sum of 3 skinfolds: _____ mm % body fat: _____ % Rating: _____ Circumf.: _____ Rating: _____ Ratio: _____ Rating: _____	BMI: _____ kg/m^2 Rating: _____ Sum of 3 skinfolds: _____ mm % body fat: _____ % Rating: _____ Circumf.: _____ Rating: _____ Ratio: _____ Rating: _____
LAB 8.1 Daily Diet Number of servings Number of servings Number of servings Number of servings Number of servings	Milk, cheese, etc.: _____ Meat, poultry, fish, etc.: _____ Fruits: _____ Vegetables: _____ Breads, cereals, rice, etc.: _____	Milk, cheese, etc.: _____ Meat, poultry, fish, etc.: _____ Fruits: _____ Vegetables: _____ Breads, cereals, rice, etc.: _____
LAB 8.2 Dietary Analysis Percentage of calories Percentage of calories Percentage of calories Percentage of calories	From protein: _____% From fat: _____% From saturated fat: _____% From carbohydrate: _____%	From protein: _____% From fat: _____% From saturated fat: _____% From carbohydrate: _____%
LAB 9.1 Daily Energy Needs	Daily energy needs: _____ cal/day	Daily energy needs: _____ cal/day
LAB 10.1 Identifying Stressors	Average weekly stress score: _____	Average weekly stress score: _____
LAB 11.1 Cardiovascular Health CVD risk assessment Hostility assessment	Score: _____ Estimated risk: _____ Score: _____ Rating: _____	Score: _____ Estimated risk: _____ Score: _____ Rating: _____
LAB 12.1 Cancer Prevention Diet: Number of servings Skin cancer	Fruits/vegetables: _____ Score: _____ Risk: _____	Fruits/vegetables: _____ Score: _____ Risk: _____

INDEX

Boldface numbers indicate pages on which glossary definitions appear.